D0460907

RANGER RICK'S BEST FRIENDS

HI, I'M RANGER RICK, the official conservation symbol for young members of the National Wildlife Federation, and leader of the Ranger Rick Nature Clubs. On behalf of all the animals in Deep Green Wood, welcome to our world of nature and wildlife.

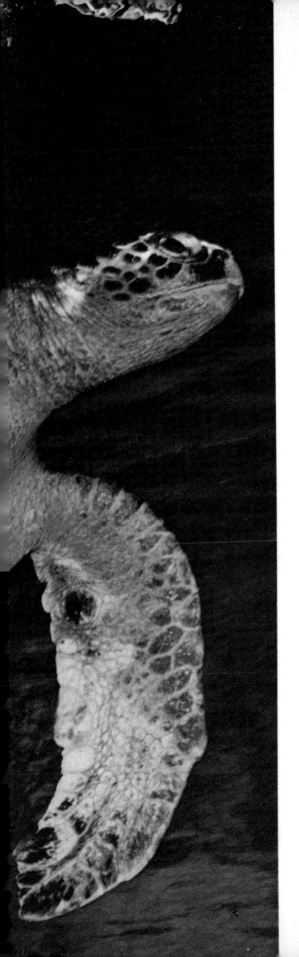

Turtles and Tortoises

by Fred Johnson

**Created and Published by
The National Wildlife Federation
Washington, D. C.**

Copyright © 1973 National Wildlife Federation
Standard Book Number 0-912186-10-0
Library of Congress Catalog Card Number 73-91357

1 Mischief at Muddy Marsh

based on characters developed by J. A. Brownridge

The sun had just come up over Deep Green Wood. Already there was a feeling of excitement as the young animals got ready for school. Today Ranger Rick was going to take them for another nature hike. But this was going to be extra special. Rick had told them that he had a surprise for them now that springtime had come.

"Wow! What a day," squealed Sammy Squirrel with delight. He scampered down his tree and ran off along the muddy path to school.

"Hey, Toby!" he called when he got near Toby Turtle's little pond. "What do you think Rick's surprise is going to be?" But there was no answer.

"Wake up, Toby, or you'll be late," Sammy called again. Then hearing nothing but the murmur of the spring breeze, Sammy turned to continue down the trail. Suddenly without warning, a green shape that looked like a rock moved out from under him. Sammy fell in a heap to the side of the trail.

"Hah! I fooled you that time, Sammy," laughed Toby Turtle. "You've got to look where you're going or you'll never get there. That's what we turtles say."

"I guess you're right," said Sammy brushing himself off. "But come on, Toby. I'll beat you to school!"

The slow-moving turtle waddled along behind. Finally he reached the crest of the hill where the path dropped down into the schoolyard. He saw that Sammy was already halfway down the hill. But, pulling his arms and feet into his shell, Toby turned himself into a cannon ball. Down the hill he rolled. Crash! He banged into the big tree in the middle of the schoolyard just as Sammy touched it. Huffing and puffing, they both agreed the race was a tie.

All the other young animals had now gathered there, too. They were chattering happily, waiting for their trip to start.

"Take your seats, everyone," called Teacher Frances Flicker as she and Ranger Rick came into the schoolyard.

"Hi, kids!" said Ranger Rick. "Miss Flicker has asked me to take you on a walk through Deep Green Wood today to look for wildflowers. I have a surprise for you, too. So let's go!"

Ranger Rick and the other animals were soon on the trail to Muddy Marsh. Everyone concentrated on each new sight: the butterflies, the fresh, young leaves, the bright wildflowers poking

their way up through the soft ground.

"Here's the surprise!" said Rick, showing them a green flower with a curious kind of hood. None of the animals—not even Toby Turtle, who knew a lot about the swamp's wildflowers—had seen one like it before.

"It's called a jack-in-the-pulpit," Rick explained. "That's because it looks like a preacher standing in his pulpit, about to deliver his sermon."

"Boy, I'd like to pick that and take it home," remarked Cubby Bear.

"No, you don't, Cubby!" Rick cried as

5

the bear started toward the flower. "That's why none of you have seen a jack-in-the-pulpit before, and why they're so seldom found in the United States. People pick the wildflowers, and the flowers can't reseed themselves—and then everyone wonders why the fields and swamps don't look pretty anymore!"

"It sure has changed around here," Toby agreed. "I can remember how pretty it used to be before the ponds started drying up."

"That's right," said his friend Sammy Squirrel. "Muddy Marsh isn't very muddy anymore. I wonder why?"

"A lot of swamps, bogs, and marshes are being drained now," Rick answered. "People think they're buggy places. Builders want to clear the land and put up more houses. Follow along the trail here and I'll show you where a bulldozer is making drainage ditches."

The young animals ran eagerly ahead. They had no sooner turned the next corner when Rick and Toby, who were at the back of the line, heard a scream up ahead. It sounded as if the class had been attacked by Wally Wolf!

Rick hurried farther along and saw Cubby sitting on the ground, looking dazed and still a bit scared. Sammy and the others were laughing at him and helping him to his feet.

"What happened?" asked Toby, who at last arrived on the scene. "Was it Wally?"

"No, it was your cousin Stanley Snapping Turtle," Sammy said. "And, boy was he grouchy!"

"Yes, he is these days," Toby admitted. "The pond where he lives is probably drying up just like mine, so maybe he was out looking for another nice, wet place to move to. Look out for him when he's on dry land; that's when he's snappy."

"Well, when he opened those big jaws and lunged, I sure thought I'd had it," Cubby said. "I just somersaulted over this log here, and the next thing I knew I was flat on my back. Now I'm all cold and wet."

"Speaking of getting wet," said Rick, "we'd better hurry along. Look at those clouds forming overhead."

When they all reached Big Bend where the bulldozer was working, Teacher Francis Flicker was nervously chattering at them from an overhead tree. "Hurry along and get back to school, or you'll all be good and wet!"

Soon the drops began to fall.

"Goodbye, Rick" said Toby. "I'm going to stay here and enjoy this. The rain sounds great on the top of my shell. I'll just settle down inside here and pray that the rain washes that bulldozer away."

"This little shower won't do that, Toby," Rick answered. "But maybe if the Rangers tell people in other neighborhoods how much harm changing the landscape can do, that might help save your swamp."

"I hope the Rangers can help, Rick," Toby said, beginning to pull in his arms and legs. "Please do what you can. We turtles have a lot of tricks that help us survive, but we can't survive if people don't care about us."

"OK, Toby," Rick answered, waving goodby. "It's been fun hearing about you and your swamp, and interesting to learn about your cousin Stanley, too. I'm sure our Rangers will want to read more about turtles in the next chapters of this book."

2 Spring Calls Pokey

In a small, sunny spot beside the stone wall, last year's leaves are stirring. There is no breeze. No small creature is scurrying by. Yet something's rustling; something seems to be pushing up from underneath!

The leaves part, and a horny, hooked beak appears. Two round, brown eyes peer about. Then a wrinkled, skinny neck appears and a fat, clawed foot reaches out.

It's Pokey Box Turtle coming out of hibernation, shaking off her long winter sleep.

In coming out she pushed a worm out of the ground. It squirmed to get back in but Pokey saw it. She grabbed the wriggler and gulped it down. It was a welcome snack after so many months of no food.

Presently she began to lumber off. Her keen eyes had seen a patch of new clover not far away. On the

Her winter nap ended, the box turtle digs out to greet spring.

8

Which way's the pond? The turtle sticks her neck out to find food.

way, a grasshopper came too close. Pokey snatched it.

Dirt and leaves that had stuck to her high-arched top shell began to fall off. Her shell shone in the sun—a beautiful brown, black, and orange.

This caught the eye of a wandering raccoon who had to come investigate. Pokey hissed a warning and pulled back into her horny covering.

She could do this better than turtles of other kinds because her bottom shell had a hinge that ran across her chest. This let her close up the front completely to protect her head and neck. Her legs and tail disappeared neatly into the rest of her "house."

The raccoon knew about turtles, but it hoped that maybe this time it could get that thing open. It prodded and pried at Pokey's shells and rolled her over onto her back. She simply stayed tightly inside.

Finally the raccoon lost interest and scampered off to find an easier meal. When Pokey thought that all was clear, she stuck her neck out and arched it backward toward the ground. Then by pushing with her head she managed to turn herself right side up again. It was quite a struggle, but Pokey calmly looked around for the clover patch again and headed for it. This time she got there and had her first full meal of the season.

Eating took up all of her time for

A hungry raccoon approaches. The wary turtle locks him out by bending the hinged lower floor of her house up against the roof. Don't bother to knock!

Danger gone, the brown-eyed female meets a friendly, red-eyed male.

the next several weeks. Then came an adventure.

One day in May, Pokey found an old rotted log with loads of fat grubs in and on it. She was gobbling them when suddenly, from around the other end of the log, came another turtle!

This one was not quite so big as Pokey, but the shell glowed handsomely in the sun. There was a stylish spot of mud on the fine hooked beak. And best of all, the eyes were a handsome red: The turtle was plainly a male!

They eyed each other for a while, then both began to devour the grub population of the log. As they chomped, they gradually drew closer.

After a time they nuzzled each other, head to head, beak to beak.

They paused often to clank their shells. They enjoyed the warm sun and gentle rain of May and mated. Then Pokey's friend left.

Sometime in July Pokey began to check various places in the ground very carefully. One day she found a spot that suited her.

She dug a hole about the size of her shell and about four inches deep. Here she deposited seven eggs, each football-shaped and a bit smaller than a golf ball. She covered them with dirt and dragged her shell over the place to hide the digging marks. She then wandered off, never to return.

One to get ready—digging a hole.
Two to go—laying eggs.
Three—on her way again.

Pokey's first clutch of eggs did not hatch. A skunk claimed them for dinner. Later she laid a second batch—and left these too. A snake gobbled them up.

One final set of eggs lay undisturbed, and hatched in the warm sun. But Pokey, of course, had already gone off on another picnic.

Suddenly she felt a chill. It was mid-September, but it already felt like late fall. Never in all her five years had it felt so cold so early.

She poked around in the leaves. With a bit of wriggling and digging, Pokey settled deep down for her long winter's nap.

13

Turtle Talk

One summer turtles in the Chesapeake and Ohio Canal near Washington, D.C. found themselves suddenly in trouble. Some locks of the canal were being drained and the turtles were left high and dry—almost.

A boy named Fred Hoke sped to their rescue. He knew that what the reptiles needed was a new home where they would have plenty of water, food to eat, and protection from raccoons and other predators.

For the big turtles, Fred and his brothers and sister built an outdoor refuge. They dug and cemented a small pond, then coated it with latex swimming pool paint to protect the turtles from scrapes.

In the pond they set water hyacinths and other plants. And Fred saw to it that the turtles could climb out of the water easily to a safe place to sun and dry. The airing is essential to their health.

For the smaller turtles they set up plastic tubs filled with water and added rocks, dirt, and small logs for basking. Heaters, lamps and a special filter system kept the new homes clean and comfortable.

The refugee turtles learned to eat bits of uncooked hamburger and fresh leafy vegetables. A little raw fish was a special treat. Before long, the turtles were eating from their rescuers' fingers. But you may be sure that Fred knew to wash well if he handled his turtles. Even a seemingly healthy turtle can transmit disease.

In winter turtles need special care. If it gets too cold when they are out on their own, they will burrow under leaves and dirt and go to sleep. Fred was concerned also about the hot dry days in summer. He made sure

At left, Frank Hoke, a slider in his hand, talks turtle then feeds a hungry diamondback. Above, Frank and Bonnie watch a box turtle climb a log in the rescue pool. Later, sliders, spotted turtles, and diamondback terrapins crowd the log.

there was a muddy place where turtles could dig to stay cool.

When the canal was filled again in the spring, the turtles were taken back. It didn't take them long to become wild again.

15

3 Giants of Land and Sea

LAND TORTOISES of tremendous size were discovered four hundred years ago by Spanish explorers on remote volcanic islands off the coast of South America. These land turtles were not so gigantic as the turtles that lived on earth in the days of the dinosaurs, but they were the biggest the Spaniards had ever seen.

Because there were hundreds of thousands of these huge armored reptiles on the islands, the Spaniards named the land Galapagos (gah-LA-pa-gos)—which means "tortoises."

The big animals, four to five feet long and about five hundred pounds in weight, also tasted good. Left on their backs below decks, the tortoises could not escape and could be kept for months as a fresh meat supply.

At once the Galapagos became a favorite stop for pirates plundering the coast of South America and later for men on long whaling voyages.

Today most of the Galapagos tortoises are gone; by law, those that remain can no longer be slaughtered.

Big tortoises also once lived on the Seychelles (say-SHELL) Islands nearly 10,000 miles away in the Indian Ocean. Few are left.

Most of the Seychelles survivors are found on Aldabra, one of the most rugged of the islands. Aldabra's sharp coral defies man. And that is why the gentle giant lives on, grazing contentedly on grass and clomping about on legs like a baby elephant's.

Twin tanks: a Galapagos tortoise (left) and one from the Seychelles (below).

With scaly flippers a swift young loggerhead paddles through tropical waters.

SEA TURTLES, some of them at least, are even bigger than the giant land tortoises, but they have an easier time. They spend most of their lives floating lazily about nibbling sponges and other delicacies.

Their paddlelike flippers propel them powerfully through the water, faster than Olympic swimmers. Fastest of all are the green sea turtles and the loggerheads, who have been clocked at twenty miles per hour.

But life gets tough for sea turtles when the female goes ashore to lay eggs. Walking on flippers is not easy. Neither is carrying a four-hundred pound shell if you are used to having your body uplifted by the water.

And some weigh even more than that. A leatherback, so-called because of his leathery shell, was once caught that weighed nearly a ton. Loggerheads used to be caught that weighed nearly that much. Today few are over a hundred pounds.

Smaller, but looking more like its huge land cousin, is the ridley (to right). It has the tanklike body of a tortoise, but not the elephantine legs. The Australian flatback (below) is a pancake by comparison.

Surely, though, the most highly prized of all sea turtles is the hawksbill (next page), who roams tropical seas prying crabs out of crevices. It is from horny sections of his shell that tortoiseshell jewelry is made.

Today our mammoth sea turtles are disappearing. Do you think there is anything people can do to bring them back to our seas?

Sea-farers ashore: a ridley, (above) digging a nest; (below) an Australian flatback, nesting done.

The hawksbill seems to soar
through the sea. It wears the
most valued shell in the
animal kingdom.

4 Return of the Turtles

Can you imagine standing on a beach some moonlit night and seeing thousands of huge sea turtles paddling through the breakers to reach the shore? It used to happen every spring in Florida. If scientists succeed in a life-saving experiment they're working on now, you may be able to see great turtle fleets again.

Sea turtles spend their lives eating and resting in tropical waters. But when it is time to breed, they leave their feeding grounds and swim miles, sometimes hundreds of miles, back toward the coast where they were born. They mate at sea; then the female begins a perilous journey up onto the beach to lay her eggs.

This is her undoing, for as she struggles over the damp sand she is easy prey for man.

Green sea turtles have always had

On a moonlit night, the green turtle swims toward land.

23

After burying her eggs, the awkward and tired turtle heads seaward.

a special appeal for turtle eaters. The eggs of the loggerhead are prized for making pastry. The skins of both are sold as leather. And so today few of our sea turtles nest in Florida.

To save them, laws have been passed making it illegal to capture turtles or gather their eggs on nesting beaches. But protection is also needed from natural predators. Now research teams go out on the beaches to collect newly laid eggs and rebury them in a hatchery. About sixty days later the eggs hatch.

In some projects the hatchlings are kept for a year so that they will be strong enough to protect themselves. In others, they are turned loose at birth. This way their first rush to the sea will carry them far beyond the breakers and they will not be washed ashore again and left to perish.

Raised in hatcheries or turned loose at birth, it is hoped that the turtles will find their way back to the right beach to nest.

If the scientists' turtle-saving plan works, there will soon be new fleets of turtles surging through the breakers back to Florida's shore. The turtles will return!

24

SEA TURTLE YOUNG are lucky if they survive the first moments of their life. No parent remains on the beach to guard the eggs.

One night, where there is a nest which no man or animal has plundered, the ground begins to heave. Hatchlings, like the one here, break out of their shells. Instinct sends them hurrying across the sand on oversized flippers. The pale light bouncing off the waves draws them seaward.

A crab may seize one (below), a lizard another. A gull may snare a third. A vulture tries to claim more than his share. And hungry fish wait for the rest.

But a few survive and when they are grown, spring calls them back to the nesting beaches.

5 Danger—Oil Slick!

based on characters developed by J. A. Brownridge

Rick and Ollie raced each other down the beach. It was a brisk October morning. The sun was shining brightly.

"It's sure nice here this time of year, isn't it, Rick?" panted Ollie, a little out of breath after their run across the Carolina sand. "Look at all those beautiful ducks and geese flying south for the winter."

"It looks as though they are well on their way without much trouble this year," said Rick. "Let's head back for Theresa Terrapin's place. After all, we are her guests and she'll be wondering where we are."

"This is a great life," sighed Ollie. "I almost hate to think of going home."

"In another couple of weeks it's going to be pretty cold and bleak around here and you'll be happy to be back in Deep Green Wood," replied Rick.

On the edge of the beach they saw their friend, Tessie Terrapin, and ran over to where she lay sunning.

"We sure are glad you invited us down, Tessie," said Ollie. "It's nice to have a vacation from home and see other parts of the country."

"I'm glad you could come," answered Theresa. "It's always fun to have people come to visit."

"Oh, my," she added. "Here comes Jerry Gull. *This* visitor looks as if he's in trouble. I wonder what's wrong."

"What's the trouble, Jerry?" asked Rick as the pretty bird landed nearby.

"Hi, Rick," said Jerry. "Something strange is happening down along the marshland. The water looks funny and some of the ducks that feed there can't seem to fly. Believe it or not, they don't even seem to be able to swim right."

"Oh, come on, Jerry," laughed Ollie, "who ever heard of a duck that couldn't swim?"

"I know it sounds funny," said Jerry soberly, "but I wish you fellows would come over and see what's going on. It's right around that point and down the shore about a mile. I'll fly ahead of you to show you where it is."

"I'll swim around the point and meet you there," said Theresa, lumbering off toward the water.

"Why doesn't she come with us?" Ollie asked curiously. "It's much shorter than swimming all the way around."

"Because terrapins can swim faster than they can walk," was Rick's reply.

The two friends raced across the beach. Up ahead and over a little hill they could see Jerry Gull circling above the shoreline of a little bay.

Over the hill dashed Rick with Ollie close behind. Rick was just about to call out to Jerry when he stopped so suddenly that Ollie ran right into him. Both of them sprawled in the sand.

"What in the world did you do that for, Rick?" gasped Ollie.

"Sh-h-h-h," hissed Rick. "There's a fox up there watching the ducks. See him behind those bushes? With all the noise we made we're lucky he's so interested in the ducks."

Cautiously Rick and Ollie peered through some bushes to see if the fox had spotted them. Down below they saw their adversary still staring at the birds along the shoreline.

"He looks confused!" said Ollie in a surprised tone. "It's not like that smart old fox to be confused."

"Look at that mess in the water and you'll be confused too," replied Rick.

Looking toward the water, Ollie saw what Rick was talking about. On the shore and in the water were forms that looked *almost* like ducks. Those on shore stumbled and flopped, trying their best to fly, but their wings and bodies were covered with a black, sticky mess and they couldn't go anywhere. Those in the water struggled to stay afloat and get to shore. They, too, were covered from head to waterline with the same black, sticky stuff.

A dark film with rainbow-colored streaks spread out over the water. Along the shore, plants were covered with oil and the beach was spotted with ugly patches.

"What a sight!" cried Ollie.

"It certainly is," replied Rick. "That's what they call an oil slick."

"Where does it come from?" Ollie asked.

"Well, I don't know where *this* one came from," Rick answered grimly. "It

could have come from any one of a number of places: used oil drained from cars and flushed down sewers, a leak in a pipeline, or even a shipwreck.

"No matter where it came from, something must be done soon, or a lot of waterfowl and other marsh life will die."

"You mean the fox will get them?" asked Ollie.

"No," said Rick, "A fox wouldn't touch anything covered with that smelly, sticky stuff. Since the ducks can't fly or move about, they'll just starve to death."

"You're 100% right!" said a gleeful voice behind them. "But luckily neither of you is covered with oil so you'll do very nicely."

Rick and Ollie looked over their shoulders and froze in horror. They had been so concerned about the ducks that they had forgotten to watch the fox. Meanwhile the fox had lost interest in the oil-covered ducks and had started for another place to hunt when he caught the scent of our two friends.

With a very happy and satisfied look on his face, the fox was just about to pounce on his terrified victims when he was knocked off balance. Jerry Gull had seen Rick and Ollie's danger just in time and had flown at the fox like a dive bomber.

"Run, fellows!" screamed Jerry.

And run they did, Rick in one direction and Ollie the other. Time after time Jerry dived at the furious fox, keeping him off balance and unable to run.

Meanwhile Rick and Ollie made good use of Jerry's attack and disappeared into the bushes as fast as they could go.

They went back to Theresa Terrapin's sunning spot to lie quietly in wait for her return. It wasn't long before they saw her coming out of the water toward them with Jerry Gull close behind.

"Thanks a lot, Jerry!" called Rick and Ollie. "You sure saved us that time."

"I'm sorry I didn't see that fox sooner so I could have warned you," replied Jerry. "You were pretty careless, though, letting

him sneak up on you like that."

"You're right," said Rick. "Now what can we do for those birds we're so concerned about? They are so covered with oil they'll never live without help."

"There's not much anyone can do for them now," said Theresa. "People from the village started to arrive right after you left. They will use detergents to clean the oil off as many birds as they can, but most of them will die anyway. The villagers will also try to get rid of the oil and clean up the beach, but it's pretty well ruined for a long time to come.

"There's no cure for oil pollution yet, except time," Theresa went on sadly.

"We must keep it from happening. Maybe your Rangers will read more about oil pollution of the sea and what causes it. It ruins many beaches and kills many birds every year. Scientists and the oil producers are looking for ways to help when it does happen and governments are looking for ways to keep it from happening at all."

"We'll sure tell our Rangers about it," answered Rick. "I guess we'd better be on our way before something else happens. . . .

"Thanks a lot, Jerry. You too, Tessie."

With that Rick and Ollie began their long trip back to Deep Green Wood.

DESERT TORTOISES bur-
row happily in the dry cactus
country of the Southwest.

WHERE DO TURTLES LIVE?
They are found all over the United States
except Alaska. If you want to, you may call
those that prefer dry land *tortoises*, and
the salty ones *terrapins*, but wet or dry they
are all *turtles*.

PAINTED TURTLES roam
and sun themselves in ponds,
streams and marshes from Maine
to northern Mexico and along
several western rivers.

SPOTTED TURTLES prefer
marshes, swamps and small
shallow ponds to live in. They
range from Maine south to
Georgia and west to Illinois.

DIAMONDBACK TERRA-
PINS live along the North Ameri-
can seacoast from Cape Cod to
Mexico in sheltered, unpolluted
areas of either salt or brackish
water.

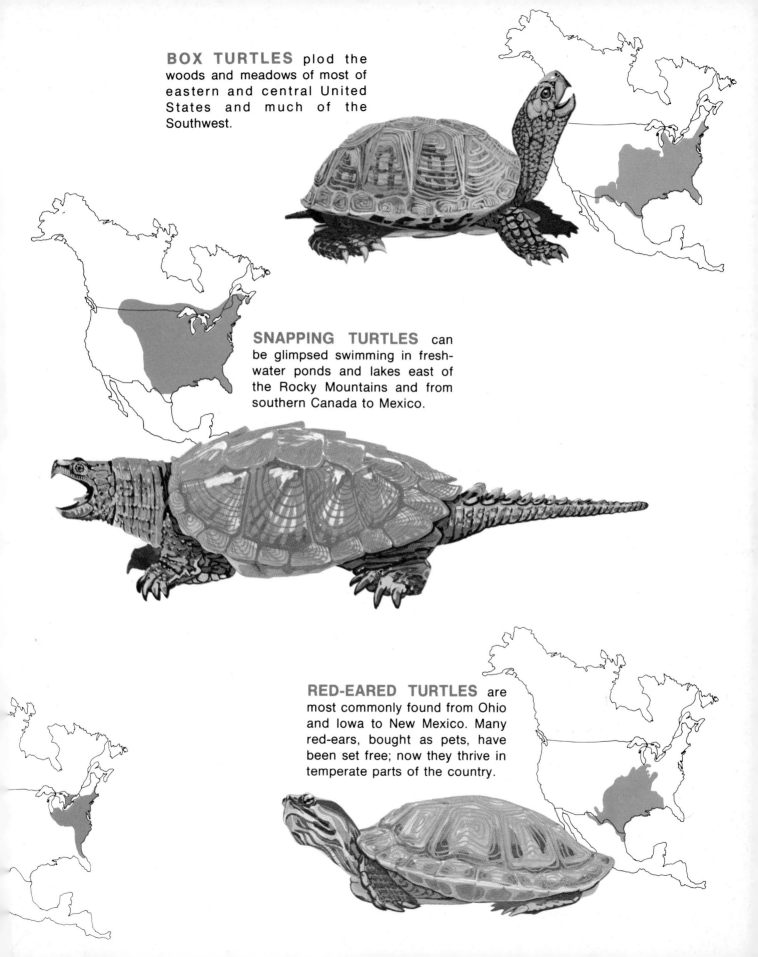

BOX TURTLES plod the woods and meadows of most of eastern and central United States and much of the Southwest.

SNAPPING TURTLES can be glimpsed swimming in freshwater ponds and lakes east of the Rocky Mountains and from southern Canada to Mexico.

RED-EARED TURTLES are most commonly found from Ohio and Iowa to New Mexico. Many red-ears, bought as pets, have been set free; now they thrive in temperate parts of the country.

WHEN YOU SEE A TURTLE...

Look closely at the double shell. The upper one, the carapace (KAR-a-pace), has lots of horny shields called scutes (below, right). Each year the scute adds a ring of growth. Count the rings. You might be able to tell the turtle's age.

Turn the turtle over. The lower shell, the plastron (below, left), is quite smooth. On a box turtle there is a hinge across the chest. This allows the turtle to pull the plastron up tight against the carapace. Then the shells fit snugly; even a piece of paper could not slip between them.

If the turtle's a male, the plastron will have an indentation.

And now, let the turtle make his way to his favorite wood to hunt for mushrooms. His stubby little legs will get him there, and his shell will protect him along the way.

CREDITS

Leonard Lee Rue III cover, box turtle, 12 (right), 32 (top); Tom Myers 2-3, Florida green sea turtle; Robert Dunne 8-9, 25 (bottom left & right); Jack Dermid 10; Harry Rogers 11 (top); John Vivian 11 (bottom), 32 (bottom left & right); Gene Frazier 12 (left); Joe McDonald 13 (top & bottom left); Nanda Ward Haynes 13 (bottom right); John Hoke 14-15; Grant M. Haist 16; Roger Tory Peterson 17; Marineland of Florida 18, 22-23; John Hyslop 19 (top right); Keith Gillett 19 (bottom); Norman Tomalin (Bruce Coleman Inc.) 20-21; Larry Ogren 24; David Hughes (Bruce Coleman Inc.) 25 (top); Victor B. Scheffer back cover, newborn Alaska fur seal. Drawings by Frank Fretz 30-31.

Ranger Rick Adventures—based on characters developed by J. A. Brownridge.

The Editors are grateful for text and picture assistance provided by the staffs of the Federation's Membership Publications—NATIONAL WILDLIFE MAGAZINE, INTERNATIONAL WILDLIFE MAGAZINE, and RANGER RICK'S NATURE MAGAZINE.

NATIONAL WILDLIFE FEDERATION

Thomas L. Kimball	*Executive Vice President*
J. A. Brownridge	*Administrative Vice President*
James Davis	*Book Development*

Staff for This Book

EDITOR	Russell Bourne
ASSOCIATE EDITOR	Natalie S. Rifkin
ART DIRECTOR	Ellen Robling
RANGER RICK ART	Lorin Thompson
EDITORIAL ASSISTANT	Nancy Faries
PRODUCTION AND PRINTING	Mel M. Baughman, Jr.
CONSULTANT	Edwin Gould, Ph.D.
	The Johns Hopkins University

OUR OBJECTIVES

To encourage the intelligent management of the life-sustaining resources of the earth—its productive soil, its essential water sources, its protective forests and plantlife, and its dependent wildlife—and to promote and encourage the knowledge and appreciation of these resources, their interrelationship and wise use, without which there can be little hope for a continuing abundant life.